Michael Jackson

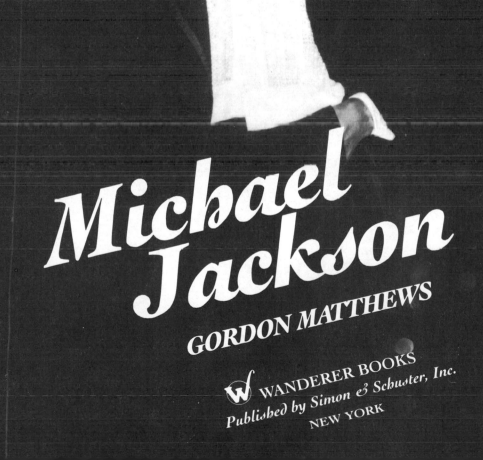

Michael Jackson

GORDON MATTHEWS

WANDERER BOOKS
Published by Simon & Schuster, Inc.
NEW YORK

This book is for Jack King Calder

Special thanks to Amy Kaplan

Published by WANDERER BOOKS
A Division of Simon & Schuster, Inc.
Simon & Schuster Building
1230 Avenue of the Americas
New York, New York 10020

Manufactured in the United States of America

10 9 8 7 6 5 4 3 2 1

Cover photograph © 1984 Dave Hogan/LGI.
Picture Credits: Joseph Stevens, Pgs. 42, 45, 55, 58, 60;
UPI, pgs. 13, 17, 23, 30, 35, 36, 40, 49; Wide World
Photos, pgs. 8, 47, 48; Jeffrey Mayer, pgs. 6, 53, 60; Laura
Levine, pgs. 26, 54

WANDERER and colophon are registered trademarks
of Simon & Schuster, Inc.
Also available in Julian Messner Library Edition

Library of Congress Cataloging in Publication Data
Matthews, Gordon (Gordon R.)
    Michael Jackson.

    1. Jackson, Michael, 1958-   . 2. Afro-American
singers—Biography. I. Title.
ML420.J175M37 1984   784.5'4'00924 [B]   84-725
ISBN 0-671-50795-8
ISBN 0-671-50636-6 (lib. bdg.)

CONTENTS

	Introduction	7
1	Getting Started	9
2	On the Road to Motown	15
3	Making It on Their Own	24
4	Michael's Movie Career	33
5	Off the Wall	38
6	A Visit to Michael's House	43
7	Michael's Special Friends	46
8	Thriller	51
9	The Future	58
10	Questions for Michael	61
	Discography	64

Introduction

He says that he cannot remember a time when he was not singing and performing. There are faded memories of the local candy store, childhood friends, and the sound of the Roosevelt High School marching band. But that was a long time ago, when he was a little kid, growing up in a house full of kids in the grimy midwestern town of Gary, Indiana.

It's been over twenty years now since his life has completely changed. That boy is now a man. Yet some of the boy remains, grasping at a childhood he never really had. Since the age of five he has been performing. "I've been doing this for so long I sometimes feel like I should be seventy by now," he recently told a reporter. A good friend described him as having "a balance between the wisdom of a sixty-year-old and the enthusiasm of a child."

Everyone in Hollywood wants to make a movie with him. Everyone in the music business wants to make records with him. He sold more records in 1983 than any other recording artist. He counts among his friends some of the most famous people in the world. He has performed for presidents and kings. He is the most popular performer in America today.

His name is Michael Jackson.

Michael at age thirteen.

ONE
Getting Started

Michael Joe Jackson was born on August 29, 1958, in Gary, Indiana. His parents, Joseph and Katherine Jackson, already had five children: sons Jackie, Tito, Marlon, and Jermaine, and daughter Maureen. After Michael came two more girls, La Toya and Janet, and another boy, Randy. It was a big brood, and money was tight in a town of widespread poverty and unemployment.

Father Joe had been a musician in the first years of his marriage. He played guitar in a local group called the Falcons. But Joe realized the band would not make the big time. With so many mouths to feed, he decided to look for a new line of work. For a time he was a crane operator. His wife worked part-time in a department store, and they were able to make ends meet. Joe's life as a musician was forgotten. Little did he know that his sons would take his love for music a step farther.

It started as a way to have some family fun. Joe would bring out his old guitar, and the family would gather around and sing songs like, "Oh Susanna," "Cottonfields," and "You are My Sunshine." When Joe was not around, the three oldest boys would sneak the guitar out of the closet. Tito was the quickest to learn, and soon the brothers were going at it, with Tito playing guitar and Jermaine singing lead vocal.

One day Joe caught Tito with the guitar. He was furious because the boys were forbidden to touch the instrument. After punishing the boy, Joe softened and asked him what he could play. The other boys sang along as Tito played. The boys nervously watched their father. They all felt relieved when Joe told them how impressed he was with their talents. Joe decided to help his sons by teaching them all he knew.

Soon the group started to take form. Jermaine learned to play the bass guitar. Then Marlon, who had been watching all along, jumped in, making the group a foursome.

But baby Michael was watching, too! When he was two years old, he shocked the family by cooing along in a near-perfect impersonation of Jermaine's singing style. It was obvious that Michael was a born leader by the age of five. His family could see his special talent, and he was elected lead singer of the group.

Now there were five Jacksons performing. A neighbor thought up their perfect simple name: the Jackson Five.

The first time Michael sang in public he knew from the audience's reaction that he had a special gift. "I still remember the first time I sang in kindergarten class," he told Robert Hillburn of the *Los Angeles Times*. "I sang 'Climb Every Mountain' and everybody got so excited."

Under their father's watchful eye, the brothers began to rehearse regularly. No longer were the boys always available to play basketball with their friends. Many extracurricular activities had to be missed. Their friends laughed and teased while the Jacksons practiced. "You'll never get anywhere," they said. "What a waste of time." But the family continued to work.

The better they got, the harder their father would push them. Joe told *Soul* magazine in 1970 how he encouraged the boys. "When I saw that they liked it, I kept them at it. I helped them when it got hard for them and when they felt disgusted as kids sometimes do. You know they like something when they find it easy and get good at it, but when they try to do harder things and they find it more work than they thought, you have to encourage them to get over that hump."

Besides practicing their harmonies and instruments, the brothers began working on dance routines. At seven, Michael was already a remarkable dancer, helping to work out moves for the whole group. He amazed his brothers and sisters.

"It was sort of frightening," Michael's mother told *Rolling Stone* magazine. "He was so young, he didn't go out and play much. So if you want me to tell you the truth, I don't know where he got it. He just knew."

In the early days, the Jackson brothers were impressed by the singer James Brown. He was a big influence on the band, especially Michael. James Brown is Michael's all-time favorite performer to this day. In the 1960s, James Brown was one of the most popular singers of soul music. His nickname was the "Godfather of Soul," because he put on such a wild, powerful show. He did lots of fancy dance steps, splits, and crazy, wiggly walks. Michael patterned his own dance routines from watching him, and the band performed a great deal of his material.

James Brown was
an early influence
on the Jackson Five.

Other sources of inspiration for the group were performers from the Motown record label. In the mid-1960s,
Motown became one of the biggest record companies in
America. Based in Detroit, Michigan, Motown made huge
stars out of a number of performers including the Supremes
(with Diana Ross), the Miracles (with Smokey Robinson),
Marvin Gaye, the Temptations, and many others.

The president of Motown Records is a hard-working
black businessman named Berry Gordy. He had once been a
boxer; later he worked in an automobile factory. Gordy
discovered he had a talent for songwriting. After he made a
little money writing hit songs for other labels, he decided to
start his own company. With only $800 he built his com-
pany into a multimillion-dollar corporation. Today Motown
Records Corporation is the largest black-owned business in
America.

The company slogan was "The Sound of Young America," because Motown made music by young people for young people. Where did Motown find these young stars? They were discovered at talent shows, on the steps of apartment buildings, singing a cappella. Many traveled to the Motown office in Detroit begging for a chance to get a start.

Pretend you are a young singer in the 1960s. You practice hard and one day you get up the nerve to go to the Motown office for a tryout. If they like you, they will put you in the Motown "charm school," where they will teach you all you need to know.

The original Jackson Five—(left to right, top row): Tito, Jackie, Jermaine; (bottom): Marlon, Michael.

Along with dance lessons and voice training, you would be taught proper etiquette at the charm school. Motown wants to make sure their future stars know how to act in public. Good grooming is also taught, right down to the proper way to brush your teeth.

Once you make it through the charm school, it is time to get some practical experience. At your first recording session, they might have you do handclaps or sing as part of a big chorus. With a little experience you graduate to background vocals. If you are good enough, it might be time to make a record.

Motown had a great number of songwriters who wrote thousands of songs in the 1960s. Only the best ones were ever released to the public. Berry Gordy would listen to all the songs and pick what he thought were the best. Then he would decide who would sing the song. Should it be a woman like Mary Wells? Or a guy and girl together like Marvin Gaye and Tammi Terrell? A band would cut the background tracks (drums, piano, and guitar—no vocals) under the direction of a producer (the person in charge of the recording session). Then, the singer would record the vocal. The person would sing it over and over again until it was perfect. The background tracks and vocal tracks would finally be mixed together. If the final results were satisfactory, the recording would be turned into a record, and you would be on the way to becoming a Motown star.

The Jacksons studied the Motown stars, their classy show costumes, and their dance routines. They even sang songs made famous by Motown artists. The Jackson Five won a talent contest in 1965 at the local high school singing the Temptations' hits "My Girl" and "Get Ready." It was the first step on their way to becoming Motown stars. But that was still five years away and there was a lot of hard work to be done first.

TWO
On the Road to Motown

Word spread quickly about the Jackson Five through the city of Gary, Indiana. Friends who had laughed at them six months earlier were now boasting about knowing the brothers. The group played in lots of talent contests and won almost all of them. The Jackson Five were in demand at block parties and functions all over the city.

Before long a local record company signed a contract with them. The group recorded two singles for the Steeltown label. Neither of the singles was very good, but one of them became a minor hit in the midwest. This allowed the Jacksons to get out of town and play at nightclubs. The Jacksons laugh when they think about what they were paid for their first nightclub performance: eight dollars!

However, there were other ways to make money. If the crowd liked them, the people would throw money. Michael and Marlon, who were the best dancers, would go out on the floor. With a spin and a split they would drop down and snatch up the loot. Sometimes they could make as much as $300 just spinning and splitting around the floor.

Michael told Jim Miller from *Newsweek* about the experience: "When we sang, people would throw all this money on the floor. . . . Tons of dollars, tens, twenties, lots of change. I remember my pockets being so full of money that I couldn't keep my pants up. I'd wear a real tight belt and I'd buy candy like crazy."

The Jackson Five were soon playing all the big cities east of the Mississippi. Marlon Jackson remembered those days when he was interviewed by the *New Musical Express:* "The good part of it was we got off school. We had just three hours of school a day, which is better than six, right? . . . It was work. We'd do the Apollo Theater and stuff, making all those runs to Chicago and Philadelphia. Seven shows a night. Me and Mike, we used to sell our photos. Can you believe that? Who would want our photos then? This is when we were working the nightclubs till four, five in the morning and be up for school by eight. Yes, sir."

When the boys played the Apollo Theater in New York City, they would open for famous stars of the day like James Brown, Jackie Wilson, and Wilson Pickett. Although Michael was too shy to talk to these performers, he watched and learned from them.

Sometimes it is tough for an opening act. You get booed and have things thrown at you by people who want to see the main attraction. The Jackson Five always won the favor of their audiences. Many of the bigger stars found out that the brothers were a tough act to follow.

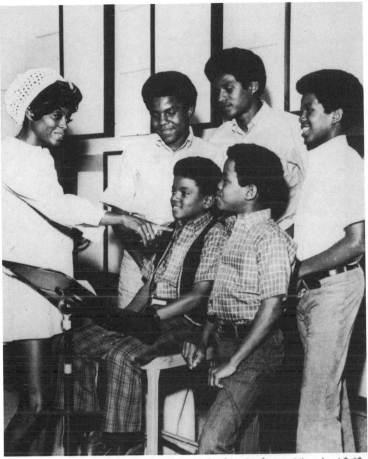
Diana Ross helped launch the Jackson Five in 1969.

Legend has it that the Jackson Five were discovered by Diana Ross. Actually, the Motown group, Gladys Knight and the Pips, played with them in 1967 and told Motown about them. Another group helped them get an audition with the label. Even though Diana Ross did not discover them, it was her enthusiasm for the group and her power as Motown's biggest star that made Motown president Berry Gordy take a closer look.

For the audition with Motown, the boys were flown to Berry Gordy's mansion in Detroit. They had never seen such splendor and it made them very nervous. Michael told *Melody Maker* about the experience: "We auditioned for Berry Gordy at his mansion in Detroit and it's really a mansion. You think everything seems big to you when you were a kid because you were so small, but oh, it's still huge. It's got everything: an indoor pool, a bowling alley, a golf course . . . we auditioned at the poolside. All the Motown stars were there. And Diana (Ross) came over and told us how much she loved us and wanted to play a big part in our career. So she introduced us to the public. Our first hit album was called Diana Ross Presents the Jacksons."

Almost immediately after the party, Berry Gordy sent the Jacksons to Los Angeles, where Motown had just moved their offices. It was time to groom the brothers for success. Berry Gordy was going to personally oversee the project. The Motown charm school was no longer in operation, so Berry had the boys move in with him in his new California mansion. Michael was the one exception. He went to live with Diana Ross. She began teaching him everything she knew about being a star.

The Jackson Five were ready. All they needed was a song that would be a hit. Berry Gordy was being very careful. He remembered how it took the Supremes seven singles and a lot of time and money before they had a hit. He wanted to find a sure hit for the Jackson Five.

One day a young songwriter named Freddie Perren came into his office with a new song. He had written the song with two of his buddies. He was hoping to get Diana Ross to record it. When Berry heard the song, he knew it would be perfect for the Jackson Five. First he made the writers go back and work on it. Berry gave them suggestions on how to make the song better. He made them change some of the lyrics, so that it would make sense for a ten-year-old boy to be singing it.

The writers worked hard on the song and brought it back to Berry. Now they had something. Berry decided that the three songwriters would become a full-time writing team for the label, and he would be the fourth member. He named the writers the Corporation.

The Corporation got the best musicians in town to cut the background track. Meanwhile, they rehearsed the boys on the vocal parts. After they recorded it, they were very proud of the results. But Berry was not quite satisfied and warned that they were getting ready to blow a sure hit.

They went into the studio again and re-recorded the song. It was late at night when they finally finished, and the young boys were ready to fall asleep. At last Berry Gordy was satisfied and the record was released. Almost before they knew it, the song was climbing the record charts until it hit number one. The song was the first of many big hits for the Jackson Five. It was called "I Want You Back."

The song was everywhere: on the radio, in nightclubs, and played in homes across the country. Everyone was going wild for the Jackson Five (J5 for short). Their first four singles all went to number one in 1970. All of them were written by the Corporation. They were "I Want You Back," "ABC," "The Love You Save," and "I'll Be There."

What made the Jackson Five so appealing to so many people? Good songs for one thing. The first four hits were all catchy songs. Once you heard them you couldn't get them out of your head. Recently, a medley of those first big hits has been released, and people who did not originally hear the songs then are picking up on them now. They sound as fresh and exciting today as they did in 1970.

When you listen to a song like "ABC," you can see why kids liked it. It was filled with fun lines about learning.

The lyrics take some basic school history and have fun with it. Michael sings about a girl who flirts with a whole bunch of guys who just happen to be famous inventors: Isaac

Newton, who discovered gravity; Ben Franklin, who discovered electricity; Alexander Graham Bell, who invented the telephone; and Christopher Columbus, who discovered America. In the song they become four boys.

Puns and wordplay were a big part of the Motown style of songwriting. The Jackson Five's next big hit, "The Love You Save," was a play on a safety slogan for drivers. "Stop! The life you save may be your own," was changed by the Corporation to, "Stop! The love you save may be your own."

The Jackson Five were the new sound of young America. Motown worked hard to make them happen. Wild, sequined bell-bottomed outfits replaced the costumes their mother had always made for them.

Motown was very protective of the group. Many early articles about them did not even include interviews with the boys. Instead, a spokesperson for Motown would speak on the Jackson Five's behalf. Lots of press was cranked out by the company, especially about Michael: "Getting to meet Michael Jackson is the secret wish of girls all over the world. Should their wish come true, they won't be disappointed. . . . Michael loves and realizes the importance of fans . . . especially the girls. He says, 'They're the ones who care the most and hope they have a chance with us.' "

Eric Williams, a lifelong fan of the J5 and currently a member of the Dancing Hoods singing group, remembers when the Jackson Five first hit. "The first time they did the Ed Sullivan show," he recalls, "I was twelve years old at the time and they just knocked me out. Michael was like a veteran already. You knew this kid was a performer. The next day at school the Jackson Five was all the kids talked about. Girls bought the teen magazines and wrote 'I Love You' over the face of their favorite Jackson. It happened overnight."

Fan mail started pouring into the Motown offices, and teen magazines cranked out a steady stream of silly stories. "Win a Dream Date with Michael!" "Jermaine Tells All!" and

"Marlon's Secret Girlfriend" were typical magazine stories. The J5 were the latest craze, just as the Beatles and the Monkees had been before them. The important fact about the Jackson Five was their being the first black group to be teen idols—not just among black kids, but among kids of every race and color. They were wholesome and cute. Even Mom and Dad could love the Jackson Five.

After the boys' first success, the family left Indiana for good. Joe and Katherine wanted to avoid the craziness of Hollywood, so they moved the family to the quiet suburb of Encino, California. The fans were not very troublesome yet, and it was possible for the boys to move around their neighborhood without getting bothered. In those days you might see the Jackson Five skateboarding or riding bikes around the town. Still, they had to avoid public places where they might be recognized.

Once the Jackson Five started making money, a variety of people started imitating them. Suddenly, there were other singing families like the Osmonds and the Partridge Family. A lot of musical ideas were stolen from the Jackson Five. But they did not get mad about it, at least not publicly. Motown had the answer, citing that "imitation is the highest form of flattery."

The Jackson Five never again achieved the kind of success they had in 1970. None of their records ever went to number one again, but they still had lots of top-ten records. "Mama's Pearl" and "Never Can Say Good-bye" both went to number two and "Sugar Daddy" went to number ten. Michael had his first top-selling solo hit with "Got to Be There." Meanwhile the boys were breaking attendance records at concerts. Eighteen thousand fans showed up at the Los Angeles Forum and 19,000 fans cheered them at Madison Square Garden in New York City.

There were numerous television appearances on such well-known shows of the time like Soul Train and the Ed Sullivan

Show. Ed Sullivan approached Michael after the group appeared on his show and told him, "Never forget that God gave you this talent." They were words that the highly religious Jackson would always remember.

Joe and Katherine made sure that fame did not go to the boys' heads. Homework had to be done and phone calls were kept to a five-minute maximum. Michael had his older brothers to keep him in line as well. As any kid brother knows, the big kids keep you in your place.

In the summer of 1971, the Jackson Five had their first TV special. It was called "Goin' Back to Indiana," and it was shot back in their old home town of Gary. The show featured Bill Cosby as a reporter trying to get an interview with the Jackson Five and Diana Ross. Because Michael's brothers were such good basketball players, they invited some of the best athletes of the day on the show to challenge them to a game. Naturally, the brothers won!

"Goin' Back to Indiana" was also the title of a new single for the group. The song lyrics included a football cheer for their old high school and the friends they had left behind.

It must have been something for the boys to return to Indiana after two years of such success. Their lives would never be the same again. How does that affect a kid? For Michael, who was shy and a little withdrawn to begin with, it was tough. To suddenly walk into a hotel and be mobbed by screaming girls may sound like fun, but it is really pretty scary. Your clothes get torn, and if you ever had someone yank hard on your hair, you know how badly it hurts.

Michael told *Rolling Stone* magazine what it felt like: "Girls in the lobby, coming up the stairway. You hear guards getting them out of the elevators. But you stay in your room and write a song. And when you get tired of that, you talk to yourself. Then let it all out on stage." That's what it's like. It is also difficult to fall in love. "With so many girls around, how am I ever gonna know?"

The Jackson Five performing on one of their TV specials on September 19, 1971.

In 1972, Michael had a number-one solo hit with a song called "Ben." It is one of his most sincere and powerful performances. Oddly enough, the song was for a horror movie about a killer rat named Ben. On the surface it sounds ridiculous, but there is an underlying message in the song about friendship.

When it seems like everyone wants something from you, it is hard to know who your real friends are. Michael Jackson desperately wanted a friend.

THREE
Making It on Their Own

The J5 machine kept rolling along. In the first three years of their stardom, over ten Jackson Five albums were released (including solo albums by Michael and Jermaine). That is more records than most bands make in a whole career! Along with all the records, there was a Jackson Five cartoon show created by the animators of the Beatles' movie, *Yellow Submarine*. There were J5 coloring books and J5 dolls. There was even a breakfast cereal with a record built into the back of the box that you could cut out and play.

As of 1983, the Jacksons were responsible for selling over 100 million records. How many records is that? To get a visual picture, figure that a stack of seventy-five albums equals a foot. First you divide seventy-five into 100 million. Divide that by the number of feet in a mile (5,280) and you get the answer. The math would look like this:

```
        1,333,333                              252
75 | 100,000,000                  5280 | 1,333,333
     75                                  1 056 0
    250                                  277 3 3
    225                                  264 0 0
     250                                   13 3 3 3
     225                                   10 5 6 0
      250
      225
       250
       225
        250
        225
         250
         225
```

You end up with a stack of albums that is 252 miles high!

The Jackson Five maintained their popularity for the first five years of their Motown career. Then, as is often the case in show business, the boys began to cool off. In the mid-1970s, their fall had started, but it was not really their fault.

Why did the Jacksons start to slip? One reason—true of many artists—was that they started to repeat themselves. After four perfect records at the beginning of their career, Motown tried to make follow-up recordings: songs that try to copy the sound of a successful record. There was "Mama's Pearl," which sounded a lot like "ABC," and "Got to Be

The Jacksons performing at Madison Square Garden in New York City.

There," an imitation of "I'll Be There." Then there was "Sugar Daddy," which was an imitation of "Mama's Pearl."

Another reason was that music was changing. Disco music was starting to become popular in 1973. It was music that was played in nightclubs, and it was designed to make people want to dance. Much of disco music used a formula of handclaps, and the constant beat of the bass drum. When Motown tried to write and produce disco songs for the Jackson Five, the results were often unsuccessful. Disco music tended to be impersonal, and a group like the Jackson Five with a strong personality just did not sound right

26

playing disco music. Years later, Michael would make disco records that worked, because he expanded on the disco formula and made it his own.

Much of the Jackson Five's problem had to do with Motown. Berry Gordy was devoting less time to his record company, putting more of his energy into making movies. One of his first big hits was *Lady Sings the Blues,* the story of the famous jazz singer Billie Holiday, starring Diana Ross.

Motown had complete control over the Jackson Five, choosing their songs and record producers. Since Berry Gordy was spending his time elsewhere, the Jackson Five suffered as a result. Many of their albums from this period were not very good. The records had "filler" tracks on them—inferior versions of songs that other artists had made popular. Motown did this with many of their performers. The version of Simon and Garfunkel's "Bridge Over Troubled Water," on the third Jackson Five album, sounded like it may have used the same background track as the version of the same song on one of the Supreme's albums.

The Jacksons were not happy with the situation. They wanted to write their own material, but Motown wouldn't let them. This was frustrating for a group with many talented members. They had worked long and hard for Motown and felt they deserved some artistic control. They looked at artists like the Beatles, the Commodores, and Marvin Gaye, who could express themselves through their own music, and they were envious.

The Jacksons certainly had not lost interest in their career even if Motown had. They pushed hard to keep in the public eye, doing many television appearances and working their first Las Vegas engagement. Many people thought the Jackson Five would bomb in Las Vegas. Instead, they put together an incredible show that set attendance records and knocked the nonbelievers off their feet. Instead of a Jackson Five show, it became a Jackson family show with sisters Maureen, La Toya, and Janet and little brother Randy joining in.

In the winter of 1973, the Jackson clan went to Africa for the first time. They performed in Senegal as part of a program to make Black American artists aware of their origins. It was an eye-opening experience for the young men who had led rather sheltered lives. They were shocked by their visit to Gorrie Island, a place where slaves were kept before they were sold off and sent to America back in the 1700s. The sight of the tiny quarters where the slaves had lived and the chains that imprisoned them made the brothers very angry. That experience had a great deal to do with their canceling a tour of South Africa in 1977. They did not want to play in a place where whites rule and blacks are treated as second-class citizens.

The year 1973 ended with the marriage of Jermaine Jackson to Hazel Gordy. Hazel was Berry Gordy's daughter. She met Jermaine when the brothers came and lived at the Gordy mansion. Their love grew as the Jackson Five's career blossomed. Berry Gordy reportedly spent $200,000 on the wedding. Many people thought Jermaine would succeed his father-in-law as the president of Motown. Everyone thought Motown and the Jacksons would continue to work happily together. No one knew how much trouble was brewing.

Some of the trouble had to do with money. When the Jackson Five joined Motown in 1968, they signed a royalty agreement. Royalties are the money someone gets from selling a record. The standard Motown royalty was 2.7 percent, or approximately sixteen cents for every record album they sold at a list price of $5.98. If a group sold ten albums, they made $1.60. If they sold a million albums, they made $160,000.

Sixteen cents for every record sold is not bad for a young band starting out, but the J5 had made millions for Motown and they wanted a bigger piece of the pie. They also wanted to write and choose material for their albums.

Berry Gordy's policies about money and artistic control had already cost him dearly. The Temptations, the Isley Brothers, and Gladys Knight and the Pips had all left Motown for greener pastures. In 1975, after a long, bitter battle, the Jackson Five left, too.

Motown took the Jackson Five to court. After a three-year battle, a ruling was made. The Jackson Five had to pay

Jermaine Jackson married Hazel Joy Gordy in December 1973. Miss Gordy's father is Berry Gordy, owner of the Motown record industry.

Motown $600,000 to get out of their contract. They also had to give up the rights to the name Jackson Five. The boys could no longer call themselves by that name, and Motown, if they wanted to, could form a new band called the Jackson Five.

Caught in the middle was Jermaine Jackson, who was now married to Berry Gordy's daughter. He was quite torn. He told *Ebony* magazine: "It seemed like the whole world was against me. . . . People didn't seem to realize I had two families and whatever I decided to do with my career wouldn't make me love either of them less. I wasn't choosing between families, I was choosing between record companies."

The Jackson Five changed their name to the Jacksons and signed a new deal with Epic records. Jermaine stayed with Motown to pursue a solo career. It was a sad day when Jermaine played with his brothers for the last time at a Las Vegas nightclub. Randy, the youngest Jackson brother, would take Jermaine's place. The Jackson brothers were no longer the cute little boys who had won the hearts of millions five years earlier. They were young men who wanted to take control of their futures. It did not happen overnight.

Epic was not ready to give full control to the Jacksons right away. Just as with Motown, outside producers and songwriters were brought in to work on the first two albums that the Jacksons did for Epic. Kenny Gamble and Leon Huff were the producers and songwriters for the albums. They had written many hits and helped create what was known as the "Philadelphia sound," working with such artists as the O Jays, Harold Melvin and the Blue Notes, and the former Motown group, the Isley Brothers.

Although Gamble and Huff wrote most of the material, the Jacksons were allowed to write two songs on each of the albums. The results were quite good, especially, "Blues Away," written by Michael for the first Epic album.

It became obvious by the second record that the best material was written by the Jacksons. Michael and his father met with the president of Epic and asked that the Jacksons be allowed to produce themselves. Epic agreed. For the first time in their career, after making over twenty albums, the group would be in control.

The result was the best album of their career. It was fitting that the record was called *Destiny*, because that is just what the Jacksons had taken control of in a literal sense. The big hit was "Shake Your Body (Down to the Ground)," written by Randy and Michael. It was their first original hit and it sold over a million copies.

"The past has seen producers producing the Jacksons, writing songs for the Jacksons, which we sang," Marlon Jackson told *Billboard* magazine. "We did the best we could, and we were very successful. But this is Jacksons' music."

Because the album had done so well, the company was excited about the next record. It was going to be a Michael Jackson solo album. But first Michael had to make a movie.

The 1984 Grammy Awards

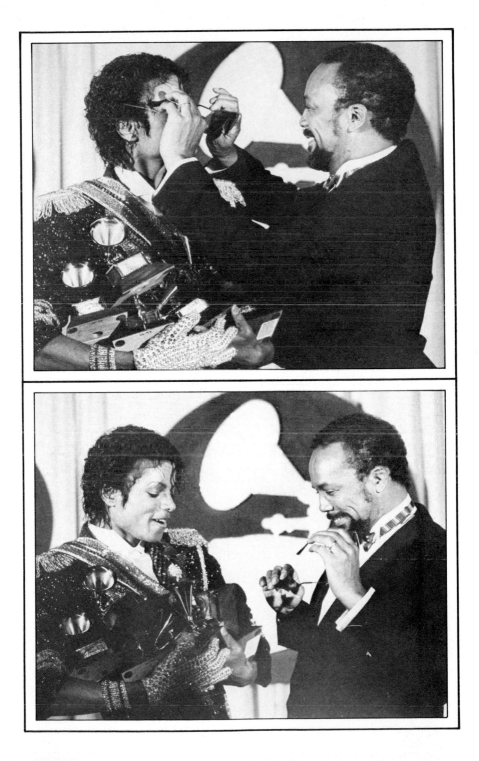

FOUR
Michael's Movie Career

When Michael was fourteen, he visited Diana Ross on the set of *Lady Sings the Blues*. He has been hooked on films ever since. Michael is what is known as a hot property in Holly-wood. Because he is such a great performer with so much star quality, everyone wants to make a movie with him. Michael is being very careful. His room at home is piled high with movie scripts. He has yet to find the script that he will commit himself to publicly.

Since *Lady Sings the Blues* he has become an avid collector of films. He especially likes films from the '30s and '40s when

Hollywood was in its heyday. His favorite is *Captains Coura-geous,* starring Spencer Tracy.

One of the first films that Michael was supposed to make was *The Frankie Lymon Story,* for Motown. Frankie Lymon was a child star in the 1950s who had a number of hit records including "Why Must I Be a Teenager in Love" and "Why Do Fools Fall in Love," a song that Diana Ross recently recorded. Unlike Michael, Frankie Lymon never made the transition to becoming an adult entertainer. He died penniless of a drug overdose. It could have been a great part with a powerful message, but when the Jacksons left Motown, the project fell apart.

Michael has acted in only one film to date. In 1977, a Broadway musical called *The Wiz* was made into a movie. The show was based on *The Wizard of Oz.* Michael played the part of the scarecrow. Diana Ross played Dorothy and Richard Pryor was the Wizard of Oz. The set for the Land of Oz was New York City and its boroughs. The yellow brick road wound its way through Coney Island, over the Brook-lyn Bridge, and into the subway system, finally reaching the emerald city, which was really the World Trade Center.

It took seven months to film the movie and Michael loved every minute of it. Michael worked hard on his part. He studied the dance musicals of Fred Astaire and the silent comedies of Charlie Chaplin to get inspiration for his scare-crow character. He became so involved with his role that he sometimes would refuse to take off his makeup at the end of the day.

Michael gained a lot of acting experience just living on the set of *On Golden Pond* in 1981. The Academy Award-winning film starred one of Michael's favorite actresses, Katharine Hepburn. Some of the films she made with her great love, Spencer Tracy, are among Michael's all-time favorite films.

Michael in 1978, promoting his
first and, so far, only film, *The Wiz.*

"I feel honored to know her," Michael told *Interview*
magazine, ". . . there are a lot of people she doesn't like—
she'll tell you right away. . . . When I first met her, I was a
little shaky because you hear things about her . . . but, right
away, she invited me to dinner that day. Ever since we've
been friends. She came to our concert—the first concert she
had ever been to. . . ."

Michael prefers doing films to being in a Broadway show.
"(Broadway) . . . it's good for sharpening your skills. It's the
best for reaching the zenith of your talent. You go so far and
reach the peak of it and you say, 'Maybe this is the best

Michael with E.T. the Extra-Terrestrial.

performance I can do.' What's so sad about the whole thing is that you don't capture the moment. . . . With film, you capture that, it's shown all over the world and it's there forever. Spencer Tracy will always be young in *Captains Courageous* and I can learn and be stimulated by his performance."

Being young forever—perhaps that is why there is talk of Michael making a movie with the famous director Francis Ford Coppola about Peter Pan, the lost boy who never grew up. *Peter Pan* is one of Michael's favorite books.

So Michael continues to look at scripts, waiting for the right movie to come along. Michael has made a storybook album about E.T. with the film's director, Steven Spielberg. He sings a song on the record and narrates the story of *E.T. the Extra-Terrestrial*. Spielberg was very moved by Michael's performance.

Michael Jackson has said he would like to write a script with Steven Spielberg. "I don't want to do anything silly," he told the *Los Angeles Times*. "I'd like to do a heavy musical drama, something with depth. Something so full of emotion that people get aroused the way they do at a concert."

Whatever Michael decides to do with his film career, he is sure to be a box-office smash.

FIVE
Off the Wall

After finishing *The Wiz,* Michael worked on his first solo album for Epic. There had been many solo albums during the Motown years, but this was the first over which he would have control. Michael chose Quincy Jones for the producer. Quincy was the musical director for *The Wiz.* He was a professional in the music industry, having worked in the business for more than twenty years. He had worked with many of the greats: Ray Charles, Billie Holiday, and Frank Sinatra. His collaboration with Michael would prove to be his greatest.

The first record they made together was one of the best-selling records of 1979. *Off the Wall* sold seven million copies. It set an industry record by having four songs from it place in the top ten.

Michael won his first Grammy Award for writing the album's first single, "Don't Stop Till You Get Enough." It is one of the greatest dance songs of all time. It also says a lot about Michael Jackson the performer. He takes control of himself and the audience when he hits the stage and the bright lights are on him. If he could, he would sleep on stage. "Don't Stop Till You Get Enough" starts with the backstage Michael, shy and hesitant, talking softly to himself while the bass guitar pulses in the background.

Suddenly, the music swells and overpowers everything. When Michael starts singing again, he sounds proud and confident, riding with the power of The Force. Michael feels the magic of the moment and the listener feels it, too.

Michael's greatest gift is his ability to communicate. "Sometimes you get a note and that note will touch the whole audience. What they're throwing out at you, you're grabbing. You hold it, you touch it, and you whip it back— it's like a frisbee."

"Don't Stop Till You Get Enough," was Michael's first number-one single since "Ben" seven years earlier. The other chart-topping songs on the album were "Rock With You" and "Off the Wall," written by Rod Temperton, and the beautiful ballad, "She's Out of My Life," written by Tom Bahler. Other great songs on the record were the dance songs Michael wrote, "Working Day and Night," and "Get On the Floor," Paul McCartney's "Girlfriend," and Stevie Wonder's "I Can't Help It."

As *Off the Wall* pushed its way to the top of the record charts, there was only one record that stood in its way. Oddly enough, that album was called *The Wall*, by the rock group Pink Floyd.

Michael at the American Music Awards in January 1980.

With the success of his album, many people thought Michael would leave the Jacksons to start a solo career. Instead, he went into the studio with his brothers and recorded a new album. For the first time, the Jacksons wrote all the songs on their record. *Triumph* was a milestone for the band. Michael made good use of the experience he gained working with Quincy Jones. He wrote or co-wrote six of the songs on *Triumph*. He also did many of the musical arrangements.

One of the best numbers is "Heartbreak Hotel," a mysterious song about a boy trapped in a scary old hotel. The music is haunting and there are lots of special sound effects. Michael's sister La Toya lets out a blood-curdling scream and there's the sound of someone falling down a flight of stairs. It is very effective, almost a movie in sound. The song was unlike anything Michael had done before. It would lead the way for material like "Billie Jean" and "Beat It."

To help promote the album, the Jacksons went on tour in 1981. The shows were the biggest and most spectacular of the Jacksons' career. Michael designed the futuristic stage set, and world-famous magician Doug Henning created all kinds of special magical effects. The tour went to thirty-six cities and sold $5.5 million worth of tickets.

Michael Hill of *New York Rocker* described the show. "What they really gave us was a fantasy, an escape, with as many thrills per minute as *Raiders of the Lost Ark*. At the heart of that fantasy was Michael Jackson, man/child with the voice of an angel . . . as the bank of stage lights rose ceilingward to reveal a large support band, Michael appeared, his willowy body draped in glittery silver and red." Michael appeared to be larger than life. "At the climax he was actually made to disappear by theatrical trickery. When he rematerialized in what seemed like a matter of seconds, he was wearing an entirely new outfit for his pop/disco classic, "Don't Stop Till You Get Enough."

Michael talked to Robert Hillburn in the middle of the 1981 tour. "It's beautiful at the shows when people join together. It's our own little world. For that hour and a half we try to show that there's hope and goodness. It's only when you step outside the building that you see all the craziness. . . . I love being on stage, but I don't like the other things that go along with touring. I didn't even want to do this tour. It was going to be canceled except we wanted to do the benefit for the children in Atlanta."

Michael relaxing after a press conference.

Because of Michael's special love for children, he felt strongly about the plight of the children in Atlanta. A number of poor children in the city were murdered by an unknown killer in 1981. The community—especially the children—were filled with fear. The Jacksons played two shows in Atlanta and donated a large portion of the proceeds to the poor families.

"One of my favorite pastimes is being with children, talking to them, playing with them," he told *Melody Maker*. "They're one of the main reasons why I do what I do. Children are more than adults. They know everything that people are trying to find out. They know so many secrets, but it's hard for them to get it out. I can recognize that and learn from it."

SIX
A Visit to Michael's House

Michael lives with his mother and father and two sisters in Encino, California. Recently, he spent $2.5 million to have the house completely rebuilt as a gift to his mother. When Michael was in England a few years ago, he fell in love with the old mansions built in the Tudor style. Some people call them gingerbread houses because they look like the house in the fairy tale, *Hansel and Gretel*. Michael had his house built in that style.

The house is surrounded by a tall fence and a gate at the driveway. There are security guards with dogs to keep people from trespassing. Kids hang around outside hoping to get a glimpse of their hero. Sometimes Michael's mother goes out and tries to talk to the kids to convince them to go home.

Inside the gates are two acres of land complete with gardens, fountains, and a lake for swans. Michael has all kinds of exotic pets, including a llama called Louis and a pair of baby deer that roam the property.

"I'm crazy for birds and puppies," Michael told *Melody Maker,* "and I love exotic things. I've had llamas, peacocks, a rhea, which is the second-largest bird in the world, a macaw, which is the largest parrot from South America, pheasants, raccoons, chickens . . . I have a wonderful relationship with animals. They really understand me. When I got my llamas, I would make this certain crazy vocabulary and they would understand and they'd come running."

One of Michael's wildest pets is a seven-foot boa constrictor named Muscles. Michael shares his pet snake with his sister Janet. Sometimes the snake sleeps in Janet's room with its head on a pillow, lying on a mattress. Michael recently brought the snake out while he was doing an interview and teased the interviewer. He told her that Muscles was trained to eat reporters!

So much work had to be done on the house that the family had to move out for a while. The new house has a room for exercise and dance, a screening room, a video arcade, and a gallery full of Jackson memorabilia. There's also a special room called the Pirate Room based on the Disneyland adventure ride "Pirates of the Caribbean." When it is finished, the room will be filled with robot pirates that rattle swords and shoot cannons.

Michael likes his own room neat and simple. It is there that he keeps his books and movie scripts. There is plenty of room for dancing.

All of Michael's older brothers and sisters moved out of the house when they got married. Even Michael's younger brother Randy, who is a bachelor like Michael, has his own place. Will Michael move out of the house soon? "Oh, no. I think I'd die on my own. I'd be so lonely. Even at home, I'm lonely. I sit in my room sometimes and cry. It's so hard to make friends, and there are some things you can't talk to your parents or family about," he told the *Los Angeles Times*.

Michael is building a place where he can feel happy and safe. A place where he can escape from the outside world and the pressure of being Michael Jackson.

Michael does not like to drive. His parents made him learn when he was twenty years old. When he does drive, he avoids the highways and sticks to roads in his neighborhood and town. He owns a Rolls-Royce Blue Silver Shadow. He uses it to travel to the recording studio, visit friends, and eat at his favorite health food restaurant called the Golden Temple.

Michael is a strict vegetarian. He is also deeply religious. As a member of the Jehovah's Witnesses, he attends services at the local Kingdom Hall. "My real goal is to fulfill God's purpose. I didn't choose to sing and dance. But that's my role and I want to do it better than anybody else."

Randy Jackson.

SEVEN
Michael's Special Friends

"I probably have two friends," Michael told *Rolling Stone* in 1983, "and I just got them. Being an entertainer, you just can't tell who is your friend. And they see you so differently. A star instead of a next-door neighbor."

Michael will not tell the names of these secret new friends. They are people with no ties to the world of entertainment. They have never even seen Michael perform. There is no pressure to be a performer with them. Michael can just be himself. They do the regular things all young people do: check out movies, play video games, and roller-skate.

46

Then there is the other group of people Michael is close to—the people he calls his "show-biz friends." This group includes some of the most famous celebrities in the world. There is Paul McCartney, the ex-Beatle who wrote the song "Girlfriend" for Michael's *Off the Wall* album. The two became very close after that and worked on more songs together: "The Girl is Mine," from Michael's *Thriller* album and "Say, Say, Say," from McCartney's *Pipes of Peace*. Michael and Paul have a lot in common. They both know what it is like to be famous with the whole world watching your every move. Also, they both love collecting old cartoons—all the Walt Disney classics and Bugs Bunny.

Another great show-biz friend is Liza Minnelli, daughter of Judy Garland. She and Michael are both great dancers,

In 1979 Michael was romantically linked with the actress Tatum O'Neal. Here they are shown dancing at a Hollywood disco party given to celebrate the ten-year success of the Jacksons.

Michael and Jane Fonda holding up their platinum record awards.

and when they get together they teach each other their latest routines. When Michael is on the West Coast and Liza is on the East Coast in New York City, they stay in touch by phone. They talk for hours at a time.

Jane Fonda is another good friend who grew up in the public eye. Her father was the famous actor Henry Fonda. She is also an Academy Award-winning actress, starring in such box-office hits as *Julia, Coming Home,* and *On Golden Pond.* Michael became close to Jane when he visited her on location for the movie *On Golden Pond,* a film she made with her father and the actress Katharine Hepburn. Michael lived in a cabin in New Hampshire where the film was shot. Jane and Michael would talk for hours about everything under the sun. Michael thought so much of her insights that he tape recorded many of their conversations.

Michael also became close to Henry Fonda and Katharine Hepburn during the filming of the movie. Jane saw many similarities between her father and Michael. Both of them are quite shy and distrustful of strangers. Michael and Henry became good buddies, with Henry teaching Michael how to fish on the lake. Shortly after the movie was released, Henry

Diana Ross with Michael in 1981.

Fonda died of cancer. Michael spent time with Jane's family in her home, sharing her loss.

Freddie Mercury, lead singer for the rock group Queen, and Michael are mutual fans. When Michael heard "Another One Bites the Dust" from the Queen album *The Game,* he convinced Freddie to make it a single. Michael was proven to be right when the song became one of Queen's biggest hits. Freddie Mercury returned the favor by making an appearance on the new Jacksons' album.

The most special show-business friend of Michael's is Diana Ross. She is the one who taught him how to cope with being a star, how to work a crowd, and how to deal with business managers. Diana worries that Michael spends too much time alone. Whenever their busy schedules permit, she tries to get him to associate with people. They go to museums and nightclubs. She recently took Michael out for a boat ride with her daughters. Michael showed his gratitude for all she has done for him by writing and producing a song for her called "Muscles."

EIGHT
Thriller

Despite the disagreements the Jacksons had with Motown, there was no denying that the business genius of Berry Gordy got them started. The Jacksons did not forget this. On May 16, 1983, along with many other Motown stars, past and present, they honored the man who had done so much for them by appearing on a television special celebrating Motown's twenty-fifth anniversary.

There were some incredible performances by Marvin Gaye, Martha Reeves, the Temptations, the Four Tops, and

Smokey Robinson. There were the Supremes, reunited with Diana Ross, but one star shined above them all: Michael Jackson.

The Jacksons' segment of the show started with a number of old film clips from various stages in the Jacksons' career. There was the original audition tape that caught the Jacksons at the very start, with a pint-sized Michael doing his best James Brown impersonation. There were clips from the Ed Sullivan Show and the Jackson Five cartoon show. Then, suddenly, the Jacksons themselves were on stage singing a medley of their biggest Motown hits. Jermaine Jackson was there to sing with his brothers. Although they are still all close off stage, this was the first time Jermaine had performed with them in five years. It was a thrill to hear Michael and Jermaine sing "I'll Be There," with the audience singing and swaying along on the chorus.

Then the brothers left, and Michael was alone on stage. "You know, I really like those old songs," he said. "But I like the new ones, too." With that, Michael jumped into "Billie Jean," and the audience screamed with excitement. Michael dazzled the studio audience and all the viewers across America as he danced, spun, and gyrated across the stage. It was as if everything he had learned in his twenty years of performing came together for those five minutes. By going back to Motown for one night, he proved just how far he had come. Michael Jackson was the ruling star of show business.

After the success of *Off the Wall,* it was hard to believe he could top it. Yet he did just that with his latest solo album, *Thriller.* It has already sold twenty-one million copies, three times as many as *Off the Wall,* and it is still going strong. The best songs on the record were written by Michael: "Billie Jean," "Beat It," "Wanna Be Startin' Something," and "The Girl is Mine." Michael received seven American Music

Michael on the Jacksons' 1981 American tour.

Awards for the record and twelve Grammy Award nominations.

The most important songs on the record are "Billie Jean" and "Beat It," because of the large numbers of people who are familiar with them. The reason for this is the crossover appeal that the songs have. "Crossover" is a term used in the music business for a record that can be played on a wide variety of radio stations. Radio stations play music in different formats. There are easy listening stations that play the kind of music you hear in elevators. There are adult contemporary stations that play love ballads. There are black music stations that play music popular in the black community, and there are rock stations that play music that is popular mainly among young white kids. Other categories are country, classical, jazz, and gospel. When a record sells a lot of copies and gets played by radio stations in different formats, the song "crosses over" and climbs into the pop charts.

Michael performing.

(Left to right): Marlon Jackson, Tito Jackson.

Jackie Jackson.

Michael Jackson had many fans when his album *Thriller* was released, but a song like "Beat It" gave him even more. Michael had Eddie Van Halen from the heavy-metal rock group Van Halen play a scorching lead guitar solo in the middle of the song. People who liked Van Halen but were not necessarily fans of Michael Jackson started buying the record for its hard rock beat. Radio stations that play hard rock started playing it. They also picked up on "Billie Jean," making *Thriller* a crossover album.

Another way that *Thriller* became popular was through the new medium of music videos. Warner Communications started MTV, short for Music Television, in 1981. The idea was to have a twenty-four-hour TV station devoted entirely to playing music. Instead of radio deejays, there were television veejays who would talk in between the video clips of groups performing their songs. It became a whole new way to sell records. New bands like the Stray Cats and Duran Duran became popular through MTV.

A problem with MTV was that they did not show many videos by black artists. They felt that their viewers, who were mainly white teenagers, did not want to see black performers. But Michael Jackson proved that they were wrong.

People loved the videos of "Billie Jean" and "Beat It." They proved it by buying more copies of *Thriller* once the videos were aired. "Billie Jean" cost $75,000 to make. The "Beat It" video cost $150,000. The most recent video, "Thriller," cost over a half-million dollars!

"Billie Jean" uses a detective theme to get the message of the song across. A detective is seen scurrying down a street looking for something. He is looking for Michael, whom he watches from around a corner. Every time Michael takes a step, a piece of the sidewalk lights up. He sees a bum sleeping in the shadows and he tosses a quarter into his beggar's cup. The cup lights up. Then the bum wakes up, surprised to find himself wearing a brand-new white suit.

Michael leans against a lamppost and the post lights up. The detective tries to take his picture, but Michael outsmarts him by disappearing into thin air! Next we see Michael singing and dancing down a long, mysterious street that stretches for miles through a dark, grimy city. The detective chases Michael into a hotel but Michael escapes by becoming invisible. The video ends with an invisible Michael running down the street, lighting up the sidewalk as he goes.

The "Beat It" video is also mysterious and exciting. Two rival street gangs meet for a rumble. One gang has a white leader and the other gang a black leader. They pull switchblades on each other and get ready to fight. Then Michael shows up and magically turns the fight into a wild dance. The video used two real street gangs and fourteen trained dancers to get its point across.

Michael gets the black kids and the white kids all dancing together. Just like he did with his album. He made music that kids of all races and nationalities love to hear.

This is something that Michael has always tried to do. On the back of the Jacksons' albums *Triumph* and *Destiny*, there is a picture of a peacock and the following message: "Through the ages, the peacock has been honored and praised for its attractive, illustrious beauty. In all the bird family, the peacock is the only species that integrates all colors into one, and displays this radiance of fire only when in love. We, like the peacock, try to integrate all races into one, through the love and power of music."

NINE
The Future

What does the future hold for Michael Jackson? Certainly a wide variety of success in many areas of entertainment are in store for him. Recently, he has written a song with Paul Anka for Johnny Mathis to record. While in England working with Paul McCartney, he also worked with new-wave synthesizer wizard Thomas Dolby. Both will contribute to each other's records. Michael is also planning to write and produce an album for Barbra Streisand.

Many people wonder if he will be leaving the Jacksons. Jermaine is planning to return to the group and Randy has proven to be a good songwriter and showperson. "I know there were a lot of rumors that Michael was through recording and touring with his brothers," Michael's father recently told the press. "After the success of *Off the Wall* and *Thriller,* no one believed he would rejoin his brothers for anything. Not so! As a matter of fact, if things go as I think they will, all my sons will be going on a world tour beginning the end of this year."

Still it is possible that Michael will leave in the near future. During the Jacksons' last tour, he told the *Los Angeles Times,* "I think it's important to grow and I've been doing this for so long. . . . It's time to move on. I still want to make records but I also want to do films. That's how I want to spend the next few years."

Performing, producing, recording, and filming. No matter how he ends up spending his time, you can be sure we have not heard the last from Michael Jackson. He is a magical performer who has not yet found all the ways to express his dreams. His star shines brightly and it is still on the rise.

The men behind the shades are Randy, Michael, and Marlon.

Michael in concert.

The Jacksons meet the press in December 1983. Michael is at the far right.

Ten
Questions for Michael

Did Michael go to school like everyone else?

In the very early years of his life, Michael went to public school, but soon the Jacksons were touring on the road, so Michael grew up with tutors. When the family moved to Encino, California, he went to a private school called the Walton School. Don't think he got off easy. His father made sure he did his homework every night.

Does he ever get stagefright?

Before a show, Michael is a bundle of nervous energy, bouncing off the walls, talking excitedly. He calls it getting pumped. Once on stage he lets it all out.

How does he spend his free time?

He does many of the activities that other kids do. He goes to movies, plays video games, and watches TV. He likes to read, dance, and draw. His artwork appears on the inside of the *Thriller* album. Two of his favorite pastimes are playing with children and taking care of his many exotic pets.

Does he smoke or drink?

Neither, and he is very opposed to the use of drugs. He told *Soul* magazine about his feelings in 1977.

"I've never tried any of those things. I'm not interested in it. I'm happy the way I am. I don't even like the word 'high.' If I want to feel free with my mind, I'll go walk the beach, read a beautiful book, or write a song. Or spend time with children, which I love to do."

How did he learn to dance?

"I've never taken a dance lesson in my life," Michael told *Ebony* in 1979. "A number of great dancers, such as Sammy Davis, Jr. and Fred Astaire, have shown me certain kinds of steps, but most of the time I practice by myself and work out my own routines."

He told *Melody Maker*, "My dancing comes about spontaneously. Some things I've done for years, until people have marked them as my style, but it's all spontaneous reactions. People have named certain dances after me, like the 'spin' I do but I can't even remember how I started the spin. It just came about."

What kind of music does he listen to?

S.O.S., Donna Summer, show tunes, Beatles, Stones, '60s music, Motown, Supertramp, folk music, classical music, old Spanish music, and lots more.

"I have all kinds of tapes and albums people would never think were mine," Michael told *Melody Maker*.

Of his own recordings, what song is his favorite?

"She's Out of My Life," written by Tom Bahler from the *Off the Wall* album, is one of his favorites. When he tried to record the song, he was so deeply moved by the lyrics that he started crying. You can hear his voice start to shake when he sings the very last word of the song.

Does he ever wish he was not so famous?

Michael appreciates all that fame has brought to him but it also brings hardships. He distrusts people whom he feels just want a piece of him. This makes it hard to make friends. He would like to be able to go to a movie theater and see a film all the way through without someone coming up and asking for an autograph.

How much money has he made?

Michael told *Ebony* magazine that, "Talking about how rich you are and standing next to fancy cars and things is tacky and tired . . . just say that we've been out there working a long time and we've been financially successful . . . well, yeah, sure we're millionaires . . . at least that, but why talk about it?"

Are his brothers jealous of him?

Randy Jackson has the answer to this question: "This girl came up to me at the hotel last night, asking if I could introduce her to Michael and saying how much I looked like him. Then she stopped and said, 'I'm sorry, I probably shouldn't talk like this. You probably don't like it when people say that.' But I don't mind at all. He's my brother and I'm proud of him. If I were a bored or unhappy person, I might be jealous. But I'm not. I'm still young. I have a lot to look forward to. We all feel like we're still growing."

Does he have a girlfriend?

He has lots of girls who are close friends. Two whom he has been romantically linked to are the singer Stephanie Mills, and the actress Tatum O'Neal. Michael brought actress/model Brooke Shields along as his date to the American Music Awards. People talk, but Michael has never admitted to being romantically involved with anyone.

Recently, Steve Manning, a long-time associate of the Jacksons, told *Right On!* that Michael does indeed have a girlfriend.

"Michael is presently involved with a young lady he cares about a great deal. However, he is doing everything he can to protect her from the glaring eyes of his adoring public. This is one thing Michael intends to keep for himself."

Who is this mysterious lady? Only time will tell.

On February 28, 1984, at the Grammy Awards ceremony, Michael Jackson set an all-time record for the most Grammy awards won by a performer in a single year—eight. They were:

> *Thriller*—album of the year
> "Beat It"—record of the year *and* best male rock performance
> "Billie Jean"—best new rhythm and blues song *and* best male R&B performance
> *E.T. the Extraterrestrial*—best children's album
> *Thriller* single—best male pop performance
> Producer of the year, with Quincy Jones, for *Thriller*

Discography

The following list is comprised of the best records made by the Jackson Five, the Jacksons, and Michael Jackson:

ALBUMS FROM THE JACKSON FIVE

1969 Diana Ross Presents the Jackson Five	Motown
1970 ABC	Motown
1970 Third Album	Motown
1970 The Jackson Five Christmas Album	Motown
1971 Goin' Back to Indiana	Motown
1971 The Jackson Five's Greatest Hits	Motown
1972 Got to be There (Michael Jackson solo album)	Motown
1972 Ben (Michael Jackson solo album)	Motown
1973 Get it Together	Motown
1973 Jermaine (Jermaine Jackson solo album)	Motown
1975 The Best of Michael Jackson	Motown
1976 The Jackson Five Anthology	Motown

ALBUMS FROM THE JACKSONS

1978 Destiny	Epic
1978 The Wiz (motion picture soundtrack)	MCA
1979 Off the Wall (Michael Jackson solo album)	Epic
1980 Triumph	Epic
1980 Let's Get Serious (Jermaine Jackson solo album)	Motown
1981 The Jacksons Live!	Epic
1982 Thriller (Michael Jackson solo album)	Epic
1982 E.T. The Extra-Terrestrial	MCA